T0165126

Module 3
Mary Magdalen's
Relationship with
Archangel Michael

K I M   C I N T I O

BALBOA.PRESS
A DIVISION OF HAY HOUSE

Balboa Press books may be ordered through booksellers or by contacting:

Balboa Press
A Division of Hay House
1663 Liberty Drive
Bloomington, IN 47403
www.balboapress.com
844-682-1282

Because of the dynamic nature of the Internet, any web addresses or links contained in this book may have changed since publication and may no longer be valid. The views expressed in this work are solely those of the author and do not necessarily reflect the views of the publisher, and the publisher hereby disclaims any responsibility for them.

The author of this book does not dispense medical advice or prescribe the use of any technique as a form of treatment for physical, emotional, or medical problems without the advice of a physician, either directly or indirectly. The intent of the author is only to offer information of a general nature to help you in your quest for emotional and spiritual well-being. In the event you use any of the information in this book for yourself, which is your constitutional right, the author and the publisher assume no responsibility for your actions.

Any people depicted in stock imagery provided by Getty Images are models, and such images are being used for illustrative purposes only. Certain stock imagery © Getty Images.

Cover Design – Saint Tone Productions.
Painting of Mary Magdalen by Kim Cintio

MaryMuntoldTRUEstory@gmail.com
Indivinetime.com

Print information available on the last page.

ISBN: 978-1-9822-7110-7 (sc)
ISBN: 978-1-9822-7111-4 (e)

Balboa Press rev. date: 09/24/2021

I dedicate this book and these teachings to every beautiful soul who has crossed my path. You have shared your message to me directly and indirectly. In turn, you gave me the drive to move forward on my journey to share the light.

To my mother, Sandra, for all your love and support throughout the years. Thank you for believing in me to make this all possible. My mom passed away prior to the completion of the book. She now watches over me and will see it all from a higher perspective.

I love you, Mom!

✍ Contents ✍

⚘ Acknowledgments ⚘

I am extremely grateful to have this opportunity to share Mary's untold *true* story of her life *in her own words*. The bond we share is indescribable. Since learning that she shares my physical body, I have felt her every emotion while writing this book and her teachings. For this, I am eternally grateful. It has been my honor to share her untold story.

To my dear brother, Steve, and nephews, Michael and Scott, for your love and support during the process of writing this book.

Janie Boisclair, my special friend. Thank you for your kindness and expertise in helping me to edit and in sharing your knowledge to assist me in the making of this book with Mary's untold story and teachings. I appreciate you!

❧ Introduction ❧

I have been a psychic medium, known as a trance channel medium, a clairvoyant (psychic clear seeing), clairaudient (psychic clear hearing), claircognizance (psychic clear sense of knowing), clairsentient (psychic clear feeling; empathy), and clairalience (psychic clear smelling) most of my life. I am delighted to share with you the direct channeling I received from Mary Magdalen herself in the hopes that it will enlighten you as to the truths about her life that have *not been told to date.*

Mary asks that you read her story with an open heart and mind to allow her words to infiltrate your being and to allow you to immerse in her truth in *her own words.* You will not find any of this material in any other form of written history or literature of any type, including the Bible, gospels, etc.

My spiritual awakening began in 2006. However, this sacred activation brought so much clarity and awareness forward for me to really understand what was coming together for my future endeavors.

In 2016, while on a sacred journey in Sedona, Arizona, I had a miraculous activation take place while I walked the medicine wheel at Amitabha Stupa Peace Park. It was there in the medicine wheel I was spiritually greeted by five sacred elder ancestors of the land. When they approached me, they cleansed me with sage, also known as smudging, as I smelled it. (Burning sage is used to cleanse a person or space of negative energy, unwanted spirits, or stagnated energies. It is an ancient spiritual ritual and a Native American tradition.) They also blessed me speaking in a language that was foreign to me. It sounded like it was in tongues or chanting like. I immediately felt the love and blessing overwhelm me. A sense of greatness was happening. They then asked me to stand in each direction while they continued to cleanse and bless me.

After they finished, I realized that something of great magnitude had just taken place. I went into the middle of the medicine wheel, stood there, looked up at the heavens with my arms outstretched, and expressed my gratitude. It was at that time that one of the women in my group came by and took a picture of me. That night, when I went to sleep, I had a vivid dream. In the dream, I saw myself with my heart wide-open and sharing massive amounts of love to the masses, including all humanity, the animal and plant kingdoms, and the world.

As I sit here writing this, I feel such an immense amount of gratitude for this amazing journey I am on. It was from this moment forward that I realized what was coming forward for me.

Through my channeling experiences, I have learned of my closeness to Mary and how she has already influenced my life.

My hope for you is to find and understand not only the truth about her journey from her own words but also how her wisdom has changed your life.

❧ Chapter 1 ❧

Who Were the Cathars?

All italicized print is Mary channeled through Kim Cintio.

The Cathars were a group of men, women, and children who lived following the practices of the teachings of Yeshua and me. They resided all over Europe, Spain, Portugal, and Italy from the eleventh to the beginning of the fourteenth century. After our time here on earth, a sacred book that had all of our teachings was put together. That book was called The Book of Love. *The Cathars followed it very strictly. They believed that men and women were equal. They lived simple lives. They were open and free-spirited. They shared what they had, fed the needy, and cared for the sick. They even provided employment in their artisan workshops. They practiced unlimited kindness, sacred love, peace, divine wisdom, and justice. They did not turn anyone away.*

They called themselves "Parfaits" or "Perfects," meaning "perfect ones." The life of a Parfait or Perfect was open to men and women to live equally. So in other words, all were treated fairly, not favoring one or the other. Those who chose to become a Parfait and a part of the Cathar community would then spend three to four years in nearby caves studying, meditating, praying, and purifying their minds and bodies. You see, my dear children, in our day and presently, it is of the greatest importance to clear one's mind and body in order to receive the incoming information from the divine. It is important to have a clear understanding of what one is receiving, to be cleansed prior to any type of transmission, in order to live their perfect lives. They held the highest respect for all souls, including the animal and plant kingdoms, coming directly from the heart space and heart center at all times. They had a great respect for all living beings and Mother Earth, which led them to be vegetarians.

You see, my dear children, during my lifetime with Yeshua, our teachings were bringing forth a new way so that all souls can live in unity and unconditional love. This is what was being brought forth then. The "New Earth" that you all have been hearing about is bringing this way of life forward once again.

Sadly, the beloved Cathars who occupied most of Europe were all part of the Albigensian Crusade. (This was the name of the group that was being exterminated by the Catholic Church because they did not follow its beliefs.) The church leaders felt they were losing control of the people. Many of the Knights Templar (refer to chapter 7 of Module 2 to learn more about them) and their family members were Cathars. The Cathars were very appealing to society, so the Catholic Church ordered all of them to be exterminated. This was Europe's first recorded genocide.

The last Cathar Perfect was burned at the stake in the castle of Villerouge-Termenes in 1321. Named Guillaume Belibaste, he uttered this prophecy,

> In 700 years, the Laurel will become green again! Good people will return. The Cathars will be back. This mysterious time has now arrived.

> The Cathars considered the Laurel to be the sacred symbol of pure love. When the inquisitors executed the Cathars, the martyrs said "The Laurel wilts. Pure love fades."

But they restored holy faith and knew that one day the Laurel would be green again.

Note: My Personal Perspective

Many of us at that time were Cathars. We have returned as the pure ones and the spiritual ones.

When I learned about the Cathars through Mary, I realized how similar my belief system is to theirs. I also continue to practice sacred love, peace, divine wisdom, and justice. I resonate with a high respect level for the souls of the animal and plant kingdoms. I do know that I was a Cathar during the 1200s to 1300s. It was when I traveled to Montsegur in southern France in 2018 that I learned I was a Cathar who had perished in the Albigensian Crusade in 1244.

When we arrived on the site, I proceeded to hike up the mountain. During that time, I had climbed about a quarter of the way up when I began to feel intense emotion, which led to me crying hysterically. I came down and began to journal.

I started channeling, and it was at that time that I learned I was a Cathar who had perished there. I sat with it for quite some time and then walked around the bottom of the mountain. While I was thinking about what had taken place, I visualized the struggle they went through while being overrun on the mountaintop, and it made me feel such sadness. I turned around and looked up at the top of the mountain, where the fortress was. I then sent healing energy up to the fortress to heal the devastating feelings left behind. To my surprise, I saw about two hundred souls come out of the trees on the mountain. I felt that they were trapped there for 774 years in between worlds.

At that moment, I sent my soul up to them and opened up the veil to assist them in crossing over. I walked through to show them the way, and they followed me. There were men, women, and children and even dogs I assisted to cross over.

After that experience, I felt so empowered. I had no idea that was going to take place. When we returned to the castle in which we were staying, I took a picture outside the window with my digital camera. In the morning, while looking at my pictures, I noticed two hundred or more orbs in the picture. These were all the Cathars I had helped cross over. I was amazed to see this.

The Universe places us in situations where we are needed, when we are needed. When something like this occurs, I do not question it. I just do as I feel I should. I knew there was a reason I had to go on this trip, and it showed itself to me when we arrived.

What experiences have you had where you have felt you were needed to change the energy of the past?

Workbook Questions

Chapter 1

Who Were the Cathars?

1. When you read about the Cathars, do you feel like you are one of them? How so?

_____

_____

_____

_____

_____

_____

_____

_____

2. Compare the lifestyle of the Cathars with your current life. Does it resonate? List all the ways and differences.

_____

_____

_____

_____

_____

3. Do you feel you were a Cathar back in the eleventh to fourteenth centuries? If yes, share your thoughts. If not, meditate and call the Cathars in to chat with you and see what transpires for you. (I recommend you journal all your experiences.)

_____

_____

_____

_____

_____

_____

4. Do you feel you can live in unconditional love and stay heart centered, without judgment of any kind to yourself or others? Can you live without fear, pain, or anger?

   Note: here is a technique that can be practiced each time you feel out of alignment, meaning not heart centered.

Place all your consciousness or focus in the center of your heart. Practice speaking and thinking through your heart. This does take practice and time. Once you have mastered this, you will be coming from a place of unconditional love. Then the rest is easy. You will notice others reacting and responding to you in a positive way.

_____

_____

_____

_____

_____

_____

_____

✌ Chapter 2 ✎

Mary's Relationship with Archangel Michael

Throughout time, Archangel Michael has been with me as my own personal guardian angel. Although Archangel Michael is not considered a guardian angel, he has been by my side during our great mission on the earth plane and in the afterlife. Archangel Michael's primary role is protection. There are many ascended masters who have important roles on the other side. Many of us work together as a team. If one of us comes to you, there is a good chance that others of us are with you also. It may not be in your awareness, but just know we are all here. You see, my beloved children, it all pertains to what is written in your soul's contract. Your soul's contract is written by you and your spirit guides prior to each incarnation. We must abide by what is written in the contract.

I often ask Archangel Michael to assist me while I do my work in the galactic realms. On many occasions, he has acted as a bodyguard to protect me from the galactic darkness. Part of my role is to help and serve galactic planets and beings of all universes. I appreciate that he is always by my side, along with other beings of light, to assist and serve.

There are many of you who are part of my team that assists me in the galactic realms during your sleep state. We travel through the universe to assist and serve and promote the light. Archangel Michael, along with other archangels, assists in the process. All the archangels are on assignment. Some of them, like Archangel Michael, have certain souls they are assigned to throughout their lifetime. Archangel Michael and I had a special bond while I was on the earth plane and still in the afterlife. However, if you would like a specific angel to come to your aid, you must call upon him or her. Because of free will, you cannot expect one to be there automatically. You must call upon one, and he or she will arrive. One will not interfere with your journey unless asked. This is the law of the universe.

Also, it is of the greatest importance when working with any light being on the other side to show your gratitude following the call. The archangels are omnipresent and can be with many souls at one time.

Kim, with whom I share a body, is one of my top students. We do many assignments together and will continue to do so for the remainder of her life, along with her twin flame.

Note: My Personal Perspective

My relationship with Archangel Michael came into my awareness during my awakening experiences as an adult. I now recognize he has always been with me because not only do I feel his vibration run through me, but I also feel gratitude to see and hear him when he arrives. How I like to work with Archangel Michael is by channeling present information about my life personally and messages for humanity. I also ask him to protect me at night while I rest. Additionally, I ask him to assist me with my healing work—and my readings and other spiritually related work. I have brought Archangel Michael in to share in my life, and in doing so, I noticed I have gained a strong sense of security because of his presence.

Have you noticed Archangel Michael's presence in your life?

Workbook Questions

❧ Chapter 2 ❧

Mary's Relationship with Archangel Michael

1. Do you feel Archangel Michael's presence around you?

_____

_____

_____

_____

_____

_____

_____

_____

_____

2. Share and describe how you feel when you notice Archangel Michael is in your presence.

_____

_____

_____

_____

_____

_____

3. How has Archangel Michael assisted you in your life?

_____

_____

_____

_____

_____

_____

_____

4. If you have noticed him in your presence, how does he make you feel when he is near you? If you have not yet recognized what it feels like to have Archangel Michael in your presence, simply ask him to come to you, and quietly see how that feels.

_____

_____

_____

_____

_____

5. The easiest way to call Archangel Michael in is to meditate.

Please feel free to converse with him as if he is a human in front of you. It will relax your conversations with him and bring you more comfort.

_____

_____

_____

_____

_____

Congratulations!

You have just completed module 3. To learn about Mary's untold *true* story and teachings, see the other modules that are available.

Module 1 - My Introduction to Mary Magdalen and How
She Came into My Awareness
Module 2 - Mary Magdalen's Current Sacred Mission
Module 4 - Nontruths Told about Mary Magdalen

Learn more, shared in detail, in the book titled *The Untold True Story of Mary Magdalen in Her Own Words*.

Printed in the United States
by Baker & Taylor Publisher Services